Mary Elizabeth Van Aulen

Home thoughts

Mary Elizabeth Van Aulen

Home thoughts

ISBN/EAN: 9783337868604

Printed in Europe, USA, Canada, Australia, Japan

Cover: Foto ©ninafisch / pixelio.de

More available books at **www.hansebooks.com**

HOME THOUGHTS.

BY

MARY ELIZABETH VAN AULEN.

CHICAGO
KNIGHT & LEONARD.
1884.

TO

MY DEAR SISTER,

THESE FEW THOUGHTS ARE MOST LOVINGLY

DEDICATED.

HOME THOUGHTS.

FATHER — MOTHER.

Names hallowed, names sacred, names never
    forgot,
  Indelibly stamped on the soul;
Names fragrant with blessing, names gentle with
    love,
  Names o'er which time's waves sweetly roll.

Names golden with beauty, with sunshine, with
    hope,
  Ne'er lost to fond memory's dream;
But breathing of music, of gladness and rest,
  Full fresh as the morning's bright beams.

I read the dear names, in each cloud and bright
    star,
  Ah yes, in the moon's quiet beam,
In the voice of the breeze, in sunset's deep glow,
  In the noise and dash of the stream.

I see them when gazing at yonder blue sky,
  And hear them in musical strain:
Dearest names of my heart, so firmly entwined,
  With memory's bright, golden chain.

Ah! fondly I linger o'er names dearly loved,
  And list, as the soft winds of even
Breathe into my spirit sweet visions of joy,
  That whisper of meeting in Heaven.

FALLING LEAVES.

Far off on mountains, distant hills,
  Upon the twilight wave,
At even-tide, amid the hush,
  Or on the lonely grave,
Or at the quiet midnight hour,
  Beneath a darkened sky,
They fall, with noiseless, gentle tread,
  Without a breath or sigh.

Amid the morning's rosy light,
  Spreading o'er sea and land,
Or noon-tide, with its gathering cloud,
  So beautiful and grand,
Or midst the storm of wind and rain,
  Or in the howling blast,
They fall in showers silently,
  In countless numbers vast.

Ah yes, they fall in lovely form,
  Of every shape and hue,
While winds oft sing in mournful dirge:
  That _we_ like leaves, fade too,—

But not forever — whispers come,
Like sweet and tender dreams,
Telling us *we* shall bloom again
Beyond life's sullen streams.

A PILGRIM OF EARTH.

I have wandered in silence, the wide world o'er,
Looking in vain for the hidden shore,
Where boat and boatman impatiently wait,
To lead each pilgrim to heaven's bright gate.
I have wandered alone, I am wandering still,
O'er mountain and valley, o'er vale and hill;
Tho' weary and thirsty, oh, bid me not stay,
A pilgrim of earth must work while 'tis day.

I've gazed at the stars, bright gems of the night,
That so brilliantly glisten in heaven's clear
    light,
For *one* that would guide me to Jordan's bright
    stream,
And light all my way with its pure, golden
    beam.
But they sparkled in beauty, not a murmur or
    sound,
From their bright starry spheres, told where
    rest could be found;
So onward I'll wander, in search of the strand;
A pilgrim of earth seeks Immanuel's land.

I've questioned the flowers that bloomed at my
  feet,
The deep-tinted rose, with its buds so complete,
White lilies, pure emblems of peace found above,
And fair blue-eyed violets, fit emblems of love.
But their bright blossoms withered without word
  or sigh;
I kissed them in silence, with a tear in my eye;
So sadly I'll wander, tho' weary and sore,
A pilgrim of earth, seeking life evermore.

I know not the depth of the dark, restless waves
Of the stream I'm in search of — how madly it
  raves!
I see not the Hand that is leading me near,
That leads me so gently, and says " never fear,
I'm with thee to guide thee o'er death's troubled
  sea;
Come, weary and sad one, oh, come unto me."
Ah, *this* shall console me, I'll lean on the Hand
That's stretched forth to pilgrims in search of
  the strand.

Then I'll put on my armor, and keep on my way,
With His hand to guide me, oh why should I stay?

With His breast to shield me, unseen tho' it be,
I'll cross the dark river; His face then I'll see,
Where bright pearly gates their doors open wide,
Where angels sit down by the soft silver tide,
Where Jesus, our Saviour, invites to His breast
Poor pilgrims of earth, seeking Heaven and rest.

NOW I LAY ME DOWN TO SLEEP.

Now I lay me down to sleep,
Dear Father, oh, my spirit keep,
And hold me in Thy full embrace,
Filling me more and more with grace;
That when the morning light appears,
I shall arise 'mid earthly fears
Refreshed, surrounded by Thy love,
Falling in shadows from above.

Yes, as I lay me down to sleep,
May angels hover near and keep
Me safe from harm, from every ill,
Fulfilling thus Thy holy will;
And when the shades of death draw near,
May every murmur, every tear,
Subside in faith, and every grace,
Parting the veil that hides Thy face.

SPRING DAYS.

In the early roseate morn,
When sweet flowers the earth adorn,
When the robin's hymn of praise
Fills the air with joyous lays,
When the sun is rising high,
Shedding warmth from yon blue sky,
Ah! *'tis then* our hearts would sing,
And welcome God's rich gift of spring,

With its genial balmy air,
With its sky of blue, so fair,
With its sweet, refreshing showers,
With its bright and lovely flowers,
With its birds of every hue,
With its sparkling morning dew.
All these comforts round us cling,
In the bright and joyous spring.

When earth's carpet, fresh and green,
Everywhere is always seen,
And the trees, in lofty pride,
Cast their shadows far and wide,

Rich with leaves of every shade,
Light and dark, o'er hill and glade,
Oh, *then* may our voices ring,
With the welcome song of spring.

Thus, sweet spring, we welcome thee,
And with faith would bend the knee,
And gratefully our voices raise,
With hymns of love and loudest praise,
To God, who sends the balmy air,
With all its blessings, rich and rare;
Yes, in our hearts we'd *ever* sing
A joyous song to thee, sweet spring.

TO A STAR.

Bright, beautiful star, rich gem of the night,
How wonderful, yet familiar to sight!
Sole watcher alone, a sentinel high,
From out the great depths of the azure sky,
Where cloud or dark shade cannot ever mar
Thy pathway of peace, oh, beautiful star!

For what have we here, so lovely and bright,
Oh, beautiful star! with soft, silver light,
In pearls from the sea, or coral's fair shrine,
In jewels most rare from out the rich mine?
Oh, nothing on earth can ever compare
With beauty like thine, so reachless and rare.

Thy power I feel, lone, beautiful star,
As I gaze to-night on thy glory afar;
Both weary and sad, my spirit would hold
Communion with thee, bright star of the fold;
I'd drink from thy fount rich lessons of love,
And list for the echo from angels above.

My soul, then, would soar, sweet star of the night,
Away to the land of infinite light,

Where songs of the blest unceasingly swell,
Where never is heard the sad word, farewell,
Where soft notes float down from Heaven's fair
    bowers,
All faint with the odor of Eden's own flowers.

Thus ever, bright star, with thy silvery light,
Look down through the depths and stillness of
    night,
And breathe to my soul sweet visions of love,
Till my heart grow athirst for glory above,
And rise as on wings, longing fondly to fly
To thy home, lovely star, thy home in the sky.

AFTER A SHOWER.

Lowering clouds have passed away,
Letting in the sun's bright ray;
Over hill and dale they play,

Brightening up the silvery stream
With its warm and genial beam,
Joyous as a summer's dream,

Leaving dewdrops on the flowers,
Sweet remains of summer showers,
All along through shady bowers.

On the hill-tops, in the glade,
On the leaf and grass, each blade,
These bright drops have lingered, stayed.

Giving tint and brighter hue,
While above, the heavenly blue
Smiles, as showers bid adieu.

Thus the earth in vestures bright,
Painted by the Source of Light,
So beautiful to earthly sight,

Leads our hearts to yonder land,
Where, on that bright and golden strand,
Are scenes immortal, true and grand.

A DREAM.

FOR ANNA AND FRANK.

I stood beside a flowing stream,
Upon whose breast a bright sunbeam
Had strayed from yonder golden sphere,
And lit upon the waters clear.

It danced in merriment and glee,
Turning its face with smiles to me,
And whispered loud enough to hear,
"A *word* with thee; dear one, draw near."

In haste I eagerly bent low,
To catch the word so *sweet* to know,
When *brighter* grew the sun's bright beam,
And lighted up the silvery stream.

Then came a whisper, soft and sweet,
With rippling murmur at my feet:
"Look down amid the watery gleam,
Thou'lt see a vision in the stream."

I looked, and ah, two faces bright
Lovingly met my wondering sight;

Faces I oft had seen before,
But now *together*, loved the more.

"With spring's fresh leaves," the sunbeam said.
"Those mirrored there will truly wed;
Their barks will sail o'er life's deep stream,
And glide where I am mostly seen.

"I'll chase the shadows from their way,
Will o'er their pathway often stray,
Will point them to the heavenly shore,
Where love's perfected evermore."

With this the sunbeam took its flight,
For yonder orb of glorious light;
I saw *no more* the flowing stream,
Or the *sweet vision* of my dream.

TO A SHELL.

Ah, rosy-tipped shell, from the far-off sea,
Thy soft moaning voice is a whisper to me,
From the waves that rise high on the white
crested foam,
Like an echo of music from out some sweet
home.
I love, yes I love, to list to thy strain,
That sweetly and softly breathes of the main.

And yet, while I list, an echo so lone
Steals over my soul, like a deep solemn tone,
For I know far away, o'er the great boundless
sea,
Are loved ones whose voices can ne'er come to
me;
Yet there is a balm that falls from above,
Wafted peacefully down, on the bosom of love.

Thus music like thine, sweet shell of the sea,
Brings out of the past dear mem'ries to me,
Which chant to my spirit, in softest caress,

And whisper fond words of the loved and the
    blest,
In soft, low-voiced moanings, so like a deep knell,
Yet with songs of the sea, from the heart of the
    shell.

NOVEMBER.

Sad month of fall, thy frosty breath
O'er hill and valley scatters death;
Bright flowers droop and fade and die,
Leaves fall and wilt, with deepest sigh.
Earth's mantle robbed of colors bright,
By touch of wintry frost so white,
While winds of piercing, chilling blast,
With whistling echoes hurry past.
  November, sad November,
   Thy voice we'll long remember.

Thy mournful, dreary days fly fast;
Thou'lt soon be numbered with the past;
Thy winds, which whistle round our door,
Will sing their midnight song no more;
For other months with colder strain
Will utter forth their notes again;
While memory oft will bring thee near,
In silent thought we'll drop a tear.
  November, sad November,
   Thy voice we'll long remember.

When evening spreads her mantle gray
O'er heaven's high arch, at close of day,
While flowers and all things round us fade
With wintry winds, and frost's cold shade,
We'll hush the ever rising sigh,
To Heaven we'll lift our eager eye;
For *there* our tears will never flow,
'Tis there that cold winds never blow.
    November, sad November,
    Thy voice we'll long remember.

TO MY DEAR FATHER AND MOTHER.

Come listen to the wintry wind, that sweeps so
    swiftly by,
And whispers with its music breath sweet tidings
    from the sky;
Yes, listen to its joyous song, as now approaching
    near
It breathes in gentle, loving tones, A Happy, glad
    New Year.

And thus the tuneful melodies in glorious anthems
    rise,
Like incense pure and holy, reaching far beyond
    the skies,
Leaving echoes clear and plaintive, that breathe
    to those most dear,
The same sweet, thrilling words of love, A Happy,
    glad New Year.

Ah yes, A Happy, glad New Year floats on the
    waves of song,
I list to catch the plaintive notes, while many
    memories throng;

Kindling beneath the magic spell, like stars of
    sable night,
O'er which my heart most fondly dwells, with
    pleasure and delight,

Tho' oft I drop the burning tear, and feel a bitter
    pain,
When looking back o'er life's past scenes, on love's
    bright severed chain,
On hope's fair vision of the past, on joy's sweet
    summer flower,
Faded and withered as the leaves, bedewed with
    sorrow's shower.

But now I listen to the song, that floats in realms
    of air,
And dream of those I dearly love, those often in
    my prayer,
And ask the Hand that blesses me, to hold them
    evermore,
And guide them o'er life's weary sea, to Heaven's
    fair, blissful shore.

Then gently as the winds sweep by, beneath cold
    wintry skies,

Tho' autumn's leaf hath fallen sere, and colder
    breezes rise,
Let hope's soft halo shine afar, oh be it dark or
    clear,
And may sweet voices ever sing, A Happy, glad
    New Year.

A Happy, joyous, glad New Year, thus may this
    hallowed morn
Be emblematical to them of Heaven's eternal
    dawn,
Where love in ceaseless rapture, like an over-
    flowing tide,
Sweeps o'er the vast expanses of the land beati-
    fied.

AIRY CASTLES.

When childhood with its graceful glee
Enthroned my spirit light and free,
I never traced the cloudy past,
But oh, imagination vast
Took my blithe spirit far away
To regions fair as flowers of May,
Where future pleasure rich and rare
Crowned all my castles in the air.

Grand schemes of innocence and joy
In golden dreams of rich alloy,
Mingling with flowers, pleasant streams
Made clear with golden fleecy beams,
Which bright and joyous kissed the sky,
Clad in rich hues that never die.
Ah these, and fancies twice as fair,
Made up my castles in the air.

But riper years my spirit clad,
Years full of youth, still oft more sad,
When thought more quiet wandered far
And pictured 'yond sun, moon and star,

Sweet strains, and voices heard before,
Now singing on the heavenly shore;
That told me, angels lingered where
Floated my castles in the air.

And oft when sunset's gentle light
Spread o'er the earth its mantle bright,
And golden foot-prints marked the sky,
Where the great sun had just passed by,
I've gazed at glories in the west,
With restless spirit, sighed for rest;
When angels whispered, "*see 'tis there,*
In yonder castles in the air."

But years have sped since those sweet hours
Of early youth, when fragrant flowers
Cast their rich leaflets at my feet,
With fragrant odors, ever sweet.
The fancies *now*, which I would clasp,
And claim as real, elude my grasp;
And so I turn in sad despair,
As *fall* my castles in the air.

And now I'd build upon a throne
A castle that will stand alone,

And bear the test of time and tide,
Leading my spirit to confide
Most fully in its wondrous power
To shelter me from storms that lower;
So *farewell*, shadows, fleeting, fair,
Farewell to castles in the air.

WILLIE.

Dear, dear little Willie,
The winds, tho' so chilly,
  Bring thoughts oft of thee;
And often at twilight,
Or by the dim firelight,
  Thy form comes to me.

And then too at midnight,
When moon and pale starlight
  Smile down from above;
Dreams picture thee nearest,
Oh Willie, my dearest,
  Sweet child of my love.

'Tis then the fond greeting,
The joy of our meeting,
  I realize again.
But oh, when I waken,
And feel I'm forsaken,
  Sad, sad is my pain.

I list in the morning,
Yes, in its fresh dawning,

HOME THOUGHTS.

For thee, my dear boy;
But hope's dreams have faded,
Thy dear face is shaded,
  And thy tones of joy.

And thro' the bright daylight,
E'en down thro' the twilight,
  I listen to hear
Thy footstep, the fleetest,
Thy voice ever sweetest,
  To tell thou art near.

Near now and forever,
When life's scenes shall sever,
  Beyond the deep sea;
Oh, may love in that hour
Bloom bright with great power
  Between thee and me.

And may we united,
Our faith firmly plighted
  To Him whom we love,
Sing ever and ever
His praises forever,
  In mansions above.

THE RAIN.

The rain comes down in gentle showers,
Watering hill tops, trees and flowers,
Mingling with rivers, pleasant streams,
Waking the calm of lakes' fair dreams,
Murmuring sweet words on ocean's breast,
In rippling music knowing no rest,
Touching the blue of the violet bright,
Lighting on flowers that bloom out of sight,
Over the mountain, on the hillside,
Down in the valley, out on the tide,
Falling from out the great fountain above,
Teaching fair lessons of faith and of love,
Pattering now on my window and door,
Making sweet music as ever before,
Excluding the rays of the sunlight on high,
Shrouding the brightness of yonder blue sky,
Casting a shadow, like twilight's sweet shade,
Deep'ning the landscape as flowers that fade,
Pattering, falling beneath all around,
Bidding bright blossoms spring forth from the
        ground,

Leading my thoughts to the fount of all love,
Who sendeth these showers of rain from above,
Filling with beauty the earth He has made,
When sunbeams creep in, dispersing the shade.

COMING FOR ME.

As I stand by the shore of the great restless sea,
  Where the tide washes over my feet,
And look far away, on the broad-reaching waste,
  Where the waves in mad glee ever meet,
I descry in the distance, almost out of sight,
  On the dark, foaming, billowy sea,
A sail with white wings, tossing wildly about;
  Oh, perhaps it is coming for me, for me,
    Oh, perhaps it is coming for me.

The waves rise in terror, the clouds droop in
    wrath,
  Still, still like a seraph at even
This ship rides the foam of the billowy deep,
  Calling loudly for aid from yon heaven.
It calls not in vain, for beyond the dark clouds
  The *voice* that stilled dark Galilee
Speaks peace to the tempest-tossed waves of the
    deep,
  And the ship rides in triumph to me, to me,
    And the ship rides in triumph to me.

The sands, wet with foam, wash the spray at my
    feet,
  While the blue of the ether above
Shines nobly upon the deep waves of the sea,
  And opens the portals of love.
I see with my spirit the wide open gate,
  Far over the deep rolling sea,
Then spread wide thy sails, white-winged vessel
    of peace,
  And say thou art coming for me, for me,
    And say thou art coming for me.

COLD DAYS.

Oh, these cold and frosty days!
How they do our poor heads craze,
With their whistling cruel ways,
    Cold, cold days.

Snow and wind, with howling blast,
Fearful in their rage fly past;
Our comfort *is* they'll not long last,
    Cold, cold days.

Sunbeams, hid by lowering cloud,
Dare not lift the threat'ning shroud,
Or stay the mighty wind so loud,
    Cold, cold days.

They linger back behind the veil,
While snow, and wind, and fearful hail
Spread over mountain, hill and vale,
    Cold, cold days,

Covering rivers, streams and lakes,
With the ice the cold air makes,
And *everywhere* with snowy flakes,
    Cold, cold days.

But bye and bye the golden beams
Will light with joy the silvery streams,
And waken us from these *real* dreams
Of cold, cold days.

THE OLD AND THE NEW.

Upon Life's ocean hangs the dear old year,
    Its dying tones I hear.
But richer, clearer, with the morning beams,
    A new year gleams,
Bidding the voyager, with steady oar,
Look hopefully for yonder unseen shore.

The old year, with its cold and misty shade,
    Says, "all things fade,"
When on the morrow, with the sun's bright ray,
    The *new* year makes its way,   ,
Pointing to brighter scenes and fairer skies,
While Heaven beams in the soul with glad sur-
    prise.

The *old* year, full of memories deep and vast,
    Of joys and sorrows past,
The *new* year with its golden, fleecy beams,
    Its fountains and its streams,
Brings us glad tidings from the land afar,
Whose glorious light is not of sun or star.

The shades of death draw heavily around
    The *old* year's funeral mound,
While out of darkness, in the stillness of the
    night,
    The *new* year heaves in sight,
Telling of joys found near the throne of light,
Where dwells our Father,— God, the Infinite.

Then swiftly speed my bark o'er Life's deep
    tide,
    My Father's hand will guide,
And safely thro' the maze of coming years,
    Dry all my tears,
That when the *old* year bids a sad adieu
The morning light may usher in the *new*.

OUR BABY.

Little gem from Heaven lent,
Little sunbeam to us sent,
Pure and guileless, fresh and fair,
Bright blue eyes and sunny hair,
Tiny hands and chubby feet,
Is there aught on earth so sweet?
Can so rich a gift be ours,
Lovelier far than fairest flowers?
Can we claim him ever thus,
Thro' sunny days and midnight's hush?
Will our baby ever be
So bright and beautiful to me?

Will he love me always so,
While the sunbeams come and go?
Will his eyes, with dancing joy,
Welcome me? the darling boy!
And with smile and sweetest kiss
Fill my heart with earthly bliss?

An answer comes within my heart,
Saying, "It is a mother's part

To love the gem upon her breast,
That fondles there for sweetest rest.
But God, who gave the precious flower,
Lends him only hour by hour.

These little ones oft catch a note
From angels, as they near them float,
And whisper of a home afar,
Where they may beam a glorious star ;
Perchance might near their parents stray
With golden gleam, to light their way.

Then, baby darling, let us pray
That God will grant thee long to stay;
That whispers from the angels bright
May not allure thee from our sight,
And that thou'lt learn a mother's love,
Ere thou shalt find that home above.

DEPARTING RAYS.

The departing rays of sunshine
  Light on the distant wave,
And touch in mellow beauty
  The shore on which they lave.
Ah! kiss the sand that glistens,
  Wet with the dark sea's foam,
And lightly smile where footsteps
  Have loved so well to roam.

They gild the tops of mountains
  Where never feet have trod,
And softly kiss the flowers
  That grow on mountain sod.
They light in tender beauty
  Upon the desert plain,
Where sands sweep ever onward
  And ne'er return again.

On shady vales and fountains,
  On distant islands fair,
On far off hills and valleys,
  They linger everywhere,—

On tower and quiet dwelling,
  On peaceful river's breast,
On tree-top where the robin
  Guards tenderly her nest.

Sweet parting rays now trembling
  With dim, uncertain light,
As creeping shadows mingle
  And bid them take their flight.
Ah, see! the rays once golden
  Have left yon mountain side,
And all is hid in shadow,
  Far out upon the tide.

But whither gone, sweet sunbeams?
  Is it to regions near?
Or hast thou gone forever,
  To bless some other sphere?
Oh, no! thou'lt come to-morrow
  To grace this world of ours,
And bless our vision with the sight
  Of earth's sweet, fragrant flowers.

THE UNSEEN LAND.

There is a land,
  All glorious bright,
Far, far beyond
  Our mortal sight.
Beyond Time's rapid
  Rolling stream,
Beyond our brightest
  Earthly dream.

We've heard sweet stories,
  Of this land
Where dwell a white-winged
  Seraph band.
We've heard of rivers,
  Fountains rare,
Of flowers that bloom
  Unceasing, there.

'Tis said eye hath not
  Seen a land
So beautiful
  With golden strand

Nor ear heard songs
  So rich with joy,
As in this land
  Of sweet employ.

No sin, or sorrow,
  Pain, or death,
Can enter there,
  With chilling breath,
Nor darkness veil
  With mantle gray,
This land where night
  Is turned to day.

'Tis there our shepherd
  Keeps his flock,
Safe from all harm,
  He is the Rock;
He leads them gently,
  Bids them rest,
The lambs he carries
  On his breast.

Beside still waters,
  Pastures green,

He guides them thro'
   The land unseen;
Clothes them in garments
   Pure and white;
Their home's with him,
   In realms of light.

Ah, when shall we
These glories see,
   And live and love,
Our God, with Thee?
   Not till the night
Of death's embrace
   Shall rend the veil
That hides Thy face.

I SEE THE WAY.

The sun had cast its last bright ray
Within a room at close of day,
Where on a couch of snowy white
 Reclined a youth, whose eye of light
Caught from the sunset's golden beam
A glimpse of heaven, the land unseen.

"Dear mother, I am near the strand,
Where saints and angels, hand in hand,
Weave garlands of immortal flowers
To crown those coming to their bowers.
Yes; nearer, nearer grows the way,
While in thy sight the sunbeams play.

Ah, let them flit about thee now;
They'll soothe the care from off thy brow;
And when I'm gone, and sunbeams grace
The room where once was seen my face,
Then, dearest mother, thou may'st know
I'm where pure, living waters flow.

I'm going now — I *see the way;*
Dear mother, bid me not to stay;

A hand so firmly grasps my own,
To lead me upward to the throne.
Dear mother, kiss me ere I go;
See! see! the heavens are all aglow."

*   *   *   *   *   *   *   *

The sunbeams' timid light has fled;
Its farewell hush wakes not the dead;
For in the arch of Heaven's bright dome
A purer light illumes his home,
A light that sheds a holier ray,
Where night is lost in perfect day.

Then dry thy tears; sad heart, be still;
Submit, and know a Father's will;
Thy child is gathered with the fold,
His feet are treading streets of gold.
He speaks in music's sweetest swell,
"*Mother*, He doeth all things well."

TO A CLOUD.

Sweet cloud, far above,
  Now tinting the sky,
With bright rosy light,
  And canopy high;
With soft, golden footprints,
  And light, fleecy wing,
So near Heaven's portals,
  Dost hear angels sing?
Ah, would I were with thee,
  Bright, beautiful cloud,
To veil the rich splendor,
  And Heaven enshroud.

Thy colors grow brighter,
  Now crimson in hue,
Tipped with gold of rare beauty,
  Against the deep blue.
While high up thou spreadest
  Like mountains of snow,
Holding guard o'er our world,
  While the soft breezes blow;

Or perhaps standing sentinel
   'Twixt us and heaven,
In robes of bright beauty,
   Sweet cloud, thou art given.

And now I would ask thee,
   Oh, beautiful cloud,
If my exit from earth
   Will be thro' thy bright shroud
To the mansions of glory
   Beyond and above?
Shall I fly, lovely cloud,
   Thro' thy pathway of love?
Shall I catch my first glimpse
   Of the land of the blest
Thro' thy veilings of cloud,
   Sweet symbol of rest?

*   *   *   *   *   *

The rays now grow softer,
   Aye fainter, in hue;
I hear only whispers
   That sound like adieu.

SHALL I KNOW THEE?

TO MY DEAR SISTER.

Shall I know thee on that shore,
The bright shore of evermore,
Where the spirit, ever glad,
In its garments white is clad?
Shall I know thee, sister dear,
In that land of holy cheer?

Shall I meet thee on that shore
Of the golden evermore,
In that land far, far above,
In that region full of love?
Shall I meet thee face to face,
In a full and fond embrace?

Yes, dear sister, on that shore
Of the glorious evermore,
Angels whisper in their song,
We shall meet mid yonder throng,
Where no more the dismal word
Of *farewell* is ever heard.

Oh, the joy, when on that shore
Of the blissful evermore,
Hand in hand, and heart to heart,
We shall meet, *no more to part;*
But with high and holy love
Praise our father — God above.

Praise Him on that glorious shore,
Praise Him ever — evermore;
Praise Him with the angel band,
On that bright and golden strand.
Sister, we *shall* meet above,
In that land of perfect love.

MY SHEPHERD.

Hark! hark! my Shepherd calleth me;
    His voice I will obey,
Tho' dark and wearisome the road,
    And rugged be the way.

Tho' snares and ills may press me sore,
    His voice shall lead me still;
Tho' night should cloud my journeyings,
    I'll know and do His will.

Hark! hark! amid the storm and cloud,
    My Shepherd's voice I hear;
'Tis sweeter than ten thousand lutes,—
    It whispers, " Never fear."

It breathes of peace and joy beyond,
    Of love — immortal love —
Where living streams forever flow
    From out the fount above.

Hark! hark! it comes in gentler strains;
    It tells of perfect rest,

For those most wearied with life's load,
  Upon the Shepherd's breast.

It clears the shadows from our path,
  It opes the gates of day;
It parts the veil, breaks thro' the cloud,
  And bears our souls away.

DREAM HOURS.

Oh, these golden hours of sleep,
When the stars their vigils keep,
And the midnight's quiet hush,
O'er the world-wide busy rush,
Stills the sighing, dries the tears,
Supports the soul beyond its fears.

Oh, these golden hours of rest,
When tired hands on weary breast
Forget life's cloudy, tangled way,
In dreams far sweeter than the day,
When all around, beneath, above,
Breathe music's gentle song of love.

Oh, these golden hours to dream
Of those we love, beyond life's stream,
Whose feet have crossed the narrow main,
Never to greet our ears again.
Still, in these golden, dreamy hours,
They come, with fragrance like the flowers.

Yes, in our golden hours of sleep,
The loved from out of memory creep,
And soften slumber's gentle chain
With words that we would hear again,
Leaving an impress, soft and sweet,
That in our dreams *our friends we greet.*

ANOTHER YEAR.

Another year, oh God! has dawned for me,
        Upon life's restless sea.
Bright, ah! and beautiful, the morning beams
        Into my window streams,
Bidding me look aloft to Thee in love,
        My cherished Friend above;

That thro' the weary maze of life's swift years,
        In all my griefs and fears,
Thy constant love has watched, to guard and
        keep
        My midnight hours of sleep,
And led me where the cloudless sunbeams play,
        To cheer me on my way.

Whence whispers come, in varied forms of love,
        From out the vault above,
Weaving bright wreaths, that promise peace and
        joy,
        Free from the world's alloy,
Where storms and angry tempests blow no more,
        On heaven's eternal shore.

Then swiftly speed my bark o'er life's deep tide,
  Thy hand will ever guide,
And safely through the maze of coming years
  Dry all of sorrow's tears,
That when life's fitful dream for me is past,
  Thou'lt give me rest at last,

Upon the shores of everlasting day,
  Scattering all clouds away,
Where, 'neath the shadow of Thy glorious cross,
  Cleansed from all earthly dross,
I shall become more like my Saviour — God,
  Within Thy blest abode.

NOT FAR AWAY.

I know it is not far, that peaceful shore,
Where my loved ones repose forevermore;
And yet the path seems long o'er life's dark way,
And faith grows weak, as shadows ever play,
>   Leaving my heart to mourn
>   Its loving treasure gone.

I know it is not far; in dreams I hear
Their voices, sweetly speaking in my ear,
And feel the loving touch, so sure to bless
And soothe the spirit with its fond caress;
>   Ah! dreams bring heaven near,
>   And wipe away life's tear.

But in my waking hours *alone* I stand,
Weary and foot-sore, in a dreary land,
Looking with eager eye far o'er the sea
For that dear land where loved ones wait for me,
>   The land that seems so far,
>   Where my *beloved* are.

"BE STILL."

My heart, my heart, "*be still*,"
  Tho' sorrows press upon thee;
For 'tis thy Father's will
  That storms shall overtake thee,
And wildly toss thy bark,
  As billows foam around thee.
'Tis His dear loving hand
  That thro' deep waters leads thee;
Thou'lt near the golden strand,
  For He'll be ever near thee.
Then, oh! my heart, "be still,"
  Thy God will guide and bless thee;
For He can with His will,
  As in the vessel with thee,
Say to the winds, "Be still,"
  And peace, sweet peace, shall greet thee.
Then, tho' the way be dark,
  My soul, thy God is with thee;
His love will break the gloom
  Of darkness that enshrouds thee;
His love will rob the tomb
  Of terrors that oppress thee.

My heart, my heart, "be still,"
  God's love will ne'er forsake thee;
But thro' the darkness, ever,
  In rays of sunlight round thee,
He'll lead thee on forever;
  His love will ever guide thee.
Then, oh! my heart, "*be still*,"
  Thy God, thy God, will save thee.